The Album of Aphorisms
A Classic Collection

The Album of Aphorisms
by Sami Frashëri

ଓଃ

Translation, Introduction & Notes
by
Flamur Vehapi

For Suhail and Nicole
who are always there for me

Table of Contents

Also by Flamur Vehapi

The Alchemy of Mind: Poems, 2008, 2016
A Cup with Rumi: Poems, 2015
Peace and Conflict Resolution in Islam, 2016
The Book of Albanian Sayings:
Cultural Proverbs, 2017
The Book of Great Quotes, 2018
Sami Frashëri's *The Expansion of Islam*
(Translation), 2019

Author's Biography

Sami Frashëri, also known as Sham al-Din Sami Frashëri,[1] was born in 1850 into a distinguished Muslim family in the village of Frashër in the district of Përmet in Albania. His father, Halit (1797-1859), and mother, Emine (1814-1861), raised and educated Sami alongside his brothers, Abdyl, Naim and five other siblings in their village as *timar* holders.[2] After the early deaths of their parents, however, Sami's older brother, Avdyl, moved his family to the City of Janina,[3] and it was there that Sami attended Zosimaia, a Greek language high school, which was one of the best educational

---

[1] In Turkish literature he is also known as Şemseddin (or Şemsettin) Sami Bey.

[2] Temporary land grant. During Ottoman times, the sultan granted lands to individuals and in return some of the revenues produced from land acted as compensation for military service. See Glossary of Terms at the end of this book.

[3] The Present-day city of Janina (Ioannina in Greek) was part of the Ottoman *Janina Vilayet* (administrative division), and its population was predominantly Albanian and Greek with Islam and Christian Orthodoxy being the major religions. Janina was ceded to Greece in 1913 following the Balkan Wars (see McCarthy's *Death and exile: the ethnic cleansing of Ottoman Muslims, 1821-1922*).

institutions in the region at the time.[4] There, Sami became proficient in French, Italian and Greek, and later learned Arabic, Persian and Turkish, in addition to his native Albanian.

It was during this period that Sami was exposed to a variety of personalities, books, and ideas on both Eastern and Western thought. With that exposure and his involvement in the local mosque, Sami was transformed into an innovative thinker, and is often rightly considered by historians as one of the leading figures in the formation of modern Albanian identity. Following in the steps of his brother Naim, in 1872 he moved to Istanbul. Sami was a prolific writer, and his achievements there flourished beyond compare. While working for the Ottoman bureau of press, he engaged in a number of local community causes and continued writing relentlessly. During this period, Sami was briefly posted in Libya (1874), and later at Rhodes (1877). He also served as chief editor for several journals and newspapers in the Empire.[5] He is famous for being known as the author of the first modern historical and geographical dictionary of the Ottoman Empire. It is said that he published well over fifty books in a variety

---

[4] See *Vepra 2*, 332-334. Also, *Kamus ul-alam*, Vol 4, 3113-3114.
[5] Gawrych, 14, 2006.

of languages, many of which are unfortunately lost today, and others have yet to be translated. Based on his accessible work and his brief biographies, one can easily conclude that Sami was a remarkable scholar and a polymath in every sense of the word.[6] Sami died in 1904 in Istanbul at the age of 54, leaving behind his wife and son. Today, just like his works, his name is well-known by Albanian-speaking communities and others around the world.[7]

---

[6] Elsie, 152, 2010.

[7] See *Great Muslims of the West* by M. Khan.

Works by Sami Frashëri

Some of Sami Frashëri's works include the following:

Drama (Turkish)

- *Besâ yâhut Âhde Vefâ* (Besa or The Given Word of Trust), 1874.
- *Seydi Yahya*, 1875.[8]
- *Gâve* (Gave the Blacksmith), 1876.
- *Mezalim-i Endülûs* (Atrocities in Andalusia), never printed.
- *Vicdân* (Conscience), never printed.

Novels (Turkish)

- *Ta'aşşûk-ı Tal'at ve Fitnât* (The Love between Talat and Fitnat), 1873.

Language studies and linguistics

- *Usûl-ü Tenkîd ve Tertîb* (Orthography of Turkish), 1886.
- *Nev-usûl Sarf-ı Türkî* (Modern Turkish Grammar), 1891.
- *Yeñi Usûl-ü Elifbâ-yı Türkî* (New Turkish Alphabetical System), 1898.
- *Usûl-ü Cedîd-i Kavâ'id-i 'Arabiyye* (New Method for Learning Arabic), 1910.

---

[8] This is a five act-play on the story of a man known as Seydi Yahya.

- *Tatbîkât-ı 'Arabiyye* (Language Exercises in Arabic), 1911.

Dictionaries and encyclopedias

- *Kamûs-ı Fransevî* (French-Turkish dictionary), 1882–1905.
- *Kamûs-ı Fransevî* (French-Turkish dictionary), 1885.
- *Küçük Kamûs-ı Fransevî* (French-Turkish dictionary), 1886.
- *Kamûs-ül Â'lâm* (Universal Dictionary or Encyclopedia of General Science), 6 volumes, 1889–1898.
- *Kamûs-ı 'Arabî* (Arabic-Turkish dictionary), unfinished, 1898.
- *Kamus-ı Türki* (Dictionary of the Classical Ottoman Turkish language), 2 volumes, 1899–1900. This work is widely used to this day.

Educational writings (Albanian)

- *Alfabetarja e Stambollit* (The Alphabet of Istanbul), 1879.
- *Abetarja e Shkronjëtorja* (The ABC Book and the Place of Writing), a work of grammar, 1886.

Scientific writings (Albanian)

- *Qielli* (The Sky)
- *Toka* (The Earth)

- *Njeriu* (The Human Being)
- *Gjuha* (The Language)

Political works (Albanian)

- *Shqipëria ç'ka qenë, ç'është e çdo të bëhet* (Albania, What It Was, What It is and What It Will Be), 1899.[9]

Other Works

In his "Pocket Library" (Turkish), Frashëri published scientific booklets on the following subjects:

1. History of Islam and Islamic civilization (such as *Medeniyyet-i İslamiyye.* Istanbul: Mihran Matbaası, 1879)
2. Astronomy
3. Geology
4. Anthropology
5. Mythology
6. Aphorisms and more.

He also published collections on proverbs, quotes, and humor, many of which are still accessible and

---

[9] Widely used by Albanian political nationalists as their "nationalist manifesto," it should be noted here that a number of sources have disputed the authorship of this work as it does not align with the teachings of Sami and the rest of his writings. First published in Bucharest, Romania, this work originally had no indication of the author or the publisher (see B. Bilmez, 2009).

referenced today in the Albanian- and the Turkish-
speaking world.

A Note from the Translator

Although a great scholar and a national prodigy, Sami is also an obscure figure in Western writings, but especially among the Albanian nationalists. He is usually misleadingly portrayed as an isolated academic and a distant national icon having nothing to do with the Ottoman ways of life, completely devoid of any religious feelings or affiliations. Such unrealistic and sterile descriptions of him suggest that the only thing Sami did in his life was ponder the glories, the suffering and the rise of the Albanian nation. Objective historians and his own life story show that these simplistic and reductionist portrayals do terrible injustice to who Sami really was.[10] Although Sami did contribute to the national cause of the Albanians and naturally did write about his beloved homeland, that was a fragment of his prolific and diverse life's work. The fact is that most of his work has nothing to do with Albania and its people, and neither were all of his works written in his mother tongue, Albanian.

First and foremost, Sami was a husband and a parent, an activist and an intellectual, a polyglot, a writer and a philosopher, a historian, a multifaceted scholar, and a

---

[10] See *Vepra 1* and *2*, 1988.

practicing Sunni Muslim, as evidenced by his own life and works.[11] Unlike popular belief, especially among the Albanian nationalists, whose rhetoric claims that no good ever came from the Ottomans in Albania, Sami never shows resentment toward the Ottomans or Ottoman rule in his homeland. In fact, according to his own writings, the Ottomans only complemented and enriched the Balkan cultures.[12] Balkan history, society and culture has certainly shown that to be true.[13]

Ë

---

[11] Some have made the case that Sami belonged to the *Baktashi* order only because the region where Sami came from Baktashism was and is prevalent. Although his brother, Naim Frashëri, in some of his writings seems to have indicated his preferences for Baktashism, Sami never hints at or gives the reader such impressions. It does appear that because of his birth region, family ties to Baktashism, and possible past affiliation with the order, by association Sami was categorized as a member, but evidence for such claims is insufficient and highly ambiguous. The Baktashi or Bektashi order is a Sufi dervish order named after a 13th century saint, Haji Bektash Veli from Khorasan, whose headquarters is in Tirana, Albania, and is mainly found throughout Anatolia and the Balkans. See, for instance, Sami's *The Expansion of Islam*, trans. F. Vehapi, 2019.

[12] See *Vepra 1* and *2*, 1988. See also *Ottoman Empire and Islamic Tradition* by N. Itzkowitz.

[13] Ibid. See also *Balkans and Islam* by A. Furat & H. Er (Eds).

In order to avoid confusion, throughout this work I will refer to Sami Frashëri as Sami or the author. All notes, citations and appendices in this work are mine. Also, all in-text comments found in parentheses are those of Sami Frashëri or the early editors/translators. The in-text comments in brackets are mine; I only added them in order to aid the reader's understanding of the original text.

Introduction

This modest work contains a little over 140 of Frashëri's numerous collections of aphorisms.[14] Most of these aphorisms first appeared in Ottoman Turkish since they were published in various Ottoman, and later Turkish, newspapers, however, a great number of them were also written in Albanian by the author, and many others were later translated from Turkish into Albanian as well as many other languages. This humble collection includes aphorisms from all of those pools, most of them being from the latter category.

Although as a translator I have edited and revised the wording of these aphorisms a number of times, I have kept the Albanian text intact in order to preserve its originality as much as possible. Therefore, those fluent in Albanian will notice some grammatical and stylistic

---

[14] An aphorism is a terse formulation of a truth, and it almost always has a twist (see *Short Circuits* by Lough and Stein [Eds.], 2018). One will notice, however, that not all of Sami's aphorisms are brief statements, as some of them can be quite wordy but I have still kept them in this collection because of the truths they contain.

inconsistencies of the original text as many of them were written in old Albanian, and others in standard.[15]

Throughout this work, I have used the author's first name, Sami, instead of Frashëri so as not to confuse him with his brothers, especially Naim and Abdyl, who are also well known in the Albanian speaking world.

I hope you enjoy this modest bouquet of wisdom by one of the most influential Albanian Ottoman thinkers of his time.

Flamur Vehapi, Translator
Portland, Oregon
October, 2019

---

[15] Note here that during the time of Sami, and even later, the Albanian language was written in both Latin and Arabic scripts. It was after 1911 that Albanians adopted the Latin script used to this day. See *Albanian Alphabets* by R. Elsie, 2017.

Author's Preface[16]

It is my hope that the small newspaper, *Sabah*
(Morning), that published many of these sayings will be
remembered for a long time because it served for me as
a way to share my writings with my beloved audience.
This paper enjoyed great popularity for some time
mainly because of a segment called *Şundan, bundan*
(therein, herein), dedicated to the entertainment of the
readers which mostly contained known and unknown
philosophical aphorisms, proverbs, and short stories.
However, when I took on a new role with *Tercüman-i
Şark* (the Interpreter of the East), another newspaper,
the readers insisted that we add a similar section there
too. Since I liked this line of work, it was my pleasure to
continue the same tradition with this paper as well,
while at the same time we shared and taught good
morals through it. Later, the publishers at *Mihran* (in
Istanbul) who were friends of mine began publishing
pocket version brochures called "Pocket Library," and
that is where some of my works were published, a few
of them being brochures of proverbs, anecdotes, and
short stories.

---

[16] This summarized preface was first published in the *Sabah*,
an Ottoman daily newspaper, on the 7th of Shaban, 1296 of
the Hijri calendar (or 1878 Gregorian) in Istanbul.

Many of my readers might be interested in knowing the origins of such sayings, so I will add a few words here to avoid any misunderstandings in that regard. It has never been my practice to adopt someone's knowledge as my own; therefore, I do not intend to take all the credit for these sayings. This collection is divided into three parts: one group is inspired by the knowledge of Western and Eastern philosophers and scholars; another group merely builds on the sayings of those wise individuals, and these are sayings that align with our values;[17] and the last group is simply the product of my limited imagination and thought which make up half of these sayings.[18] Many of these sayings reflect the time, context and the place of our society. In the event that these sayings are liked by the public, I promise that I will continue such work and publish them as time progresses, God willing.

Sami Frashëri
Istanbul, 1878

---

[17] I.e., Islamic values.

[18] In this collection, however, almost all of the aphorisms are from the latter category, unless otherwise specified in the footnotes.

The Album of Aphorisms

Faji më i madh në botë është t'i mbash anën të padrejtit e të jesh armik i të drejtit.

The greatest wrong you can commit in this life is to take the side of the unjust and become the enemy of the one who is in the right.

ℭઝ

Njerëzit nuk duhet të gjykohen nga ngjyra e tyre, por nga karakteri dhe intelekti i tyre.

People are not to be defined by the color of their skin but by the content of their character and intellect.

ℭઝ

Në vend që të shesësh dituri dhe zotësi, përpiqu t'i fitosh ato.

Instead of trying to show off your wisdom and mastery, try first gaining them.

ℭઝ

Thjeshtësia e një gruaje është më e vlefshme se stolitë e të gjitha grave të botës.

The natural simplicity (beauty) of a woman is more valuable than the ornaments of all women of the world.

 egbové

Syri është një dritare e shpirtit.
The eye is a window into the soul.

egbové

Guximi e bën njeriun të mundë luanin.
Courage helps a man defeat a lion.

egbové

Xhelozia është humnera e dashurisë.
Jealousy is the abyss of love.[19]

egbové

Dashuria është kripa e jetës, jeta pa dashuri s'ka asnjë shije.
Love is the spice of life, life without love has no taste.

egbové

Qesja nuk zbrazet duke dhënë lëmoshë.
A bag never gets empty by giving alms.[20]

egbové

---

[19] I.e., it kills love.
[20] I.e., almsgiving does not deplete one's wealth.

Vetmia është më e mirë se shoku i keq.
Solitude is better than a bad friend.

ᙍ

Këshillimi është busulla e zgjidhjes së punëve të vështira.
Consultation is the compass in resolving
difficult matters.

ᙍ

Njeriu është i lirë vetëm atëherë kur i shërben së vërtetës.
A person is free only when he serves the truth.

ᙍ

*Liria është thelbi i shpirtit dhe i mendjes. Aty ku s'ka liri,
mendja dhe shpirti thahen si bima pa ujë.*
Freedom is essential to one's spirit and thought. Where
there is no freedom, there is no thought or spirit; they
both whither like a plant without water.

ᙍ

Këmbëngulja e qëndrimi bëjnë të mundshme të pamundshmen.
Perseverance and positive attitude make possible even
the impossible.

ᙍ

Nëse do të mbjellësh për një vit, mbill misër e grurë. Nëse kërkon që të mbjellësh përgjithmonë, mbill arsim e kulturë.
If you will plant something to last you for a year, plant wheat and corn, but if you seek to plant something to last you a lifetime, plant education and civility.

ᑋ

Mendimet e larta gjenden në fjalë të shkurtra.
Thoughtful words are found in concise speech.

ᑋ

Më e bukura fjalë është e thjeshtë dhe e shkurtër, është fjalë që kuptohet me lehtësi dhe që ka kuptim të thellë e të hollë.
The best words are those that are simple, straightforward, and easily understood.

ᑋ

Njeriun e bëjnë të përjetshëm veprat e tij.
A person becomes immortal through his good deed.

ᑋ

Detyra jonë kryesore ndaj njerëzisë është të studiojmë dhe të mësojmë (të tjerët) pa u mërzitur.
Our greatest duty toward humanity is to tirelessly study and teach others.

 CB

I madh është ai njeri që i shikon të gjithë njësoj, që vepron pa anuar dhe që mendon për të gjithë. Ai që mendon për interesat e veta, është njeri i ulët.
The greatest people are those who view and treat everyone fairly, act unbiased, and think well of everyone around them. He who thinks only of his own needs is a mediocre person.

CB

Mos e duaj gjumin shumë; hap sytë që të mos mbetesh i uritur.
Do not fall in love with sleep; open your eyes and get out there to acquire your provisions.

CB

Toka mund t'i ushqejë njerëzit fare mirë; vetëm pse shumica e pasurisë shpenzohet pa vend, e shumica e njerëzve mbeten të uritur.
The earth can feed every one of us, but most of the resources that come from it are wasted and spent recklessly; as a result, many people go hungry.

CB

Për t'ia nënshtruar botën mirësisë, duhet luftuar kundër ligësive.
If we wish for mercy in the world, we first need to fight
the evils in it.

૭

*Më parë se për pasurinë, mjeshtërinë dhe tregtinë e një bashkësie
(njerëzore), duhet menduar për edukimin e saj, sepse edukata e
mirë është baza e bashkësive njerëzore.*
Before the pursuit of trade and wealth, people should
pursue education because a quality education is the
basis of a stable society.

૭

*Njeriu merret me dituri dhe me shkencë gjatë gjithë jetës së tij.
Në fëmijëri i mëson ato, në rini i vë në zbatim e në pleqëri ua
mëson të tjerëve.*
A person should always be engaged with knowledge
and the sciences. He should learn them during
childhood, apply them during adulthood, and teach
them during his old age.

૭

Zemra e njeriut të përsosur është gjithmonë e pezmatuar, por fytyra e tij është kurdoherë e gëzuar.
Sad may be the heart of a good person, but their face always radiates happiness.

෩

Po të jenë nëpunësit në dorë të personave të pazotë, po t'u mungojnë armët ushtarëve, po të mbetet pas bujqësia, mjeshtëria dhe tregtia, prapëseprapë shteti qëndron; por kur sundimtarët nuk respektojnë ligjin dhe të drejtën, nëpunësit e vegjël bëhen të pabindur dhe nuk e zbatojnë urdhrin e dhënë, kështu që populli i lë pas dorë vetitë e mira dhe jepet pas veseve të këqija, atëherë nuk ka më shpresë shpëtimi.
If employees remain at the mercy of bad employers, if soldiers were left ill equipped for battle, if agricultural development and trade declined, the state might still survive. However, when the leadership does not obey the laws and the rights of others, then even those with the most menial of jobs will disregard the rules. In this manner, society will quickly replace good habits with bad ones; it is then that there is no hope of return for a state.

෩

Mos i poshtëroni njerëzit e mëdhenj për një a dy faje të tyre, sepse diamanti sado i prerë shtrembër të jetë, është më i vlefshëm se një gur i zakonshëm, i prerë në formën më të përsosur.
Do not debase your great people for a few mistaken words of theirs. No matter how crooked a diamond is cut, it is still more valuable than any random stone cut perfectly.

ಐ

Mashtrimet e mashtruesit përballojini me drejtësi, sepse gjithçka mënjanohet me të kundërtën!
The deception of a deceiver is to be handled with justice, and that is because good is the antidote of evil.

ಐ

Njerëzit janë të njëjtë para natyrës, edukata i bën të dallohen (nga njëri-tjetri).
All people are the same in nature, it is their civility that distinguishes one from the other.

ಐ

Fjala e atij që qeshet shumë, s'e bën të qeshet asnjërin.
The words of the one who laughs excessively make no one laugh.

Duhet të shfrytëzohet mirë koha, sepse jeta nga koha përbëhet.
Time should be used wisely because life is made up of
time itself.

❧

S'ka gjë më të keqe se të përqeshurit.
There is nothing worse than ridiculing others.

❧

Virtyti i bën të dashur (me njëri-tjetrin) njerëzit e mëdhenj,
njerëzit e zakonshëm — dëfrimi dhe zbavitja, të këqijtë —
vagabondazhi dhe delikti.
Great individuals come together through their good
virtues, common people through amusement and
entertainment, bad people through foolishness
and arrogance.

❧

Pa bashkim s'mund të ketë as opinion publik, as forcë.
Without unity, there is no public opinion or strength.

❧

Duhen shumë mend që të mund të shoqërohesh me njerëz
të pa mend.

It takes tremendous willpower and intellect to associate
with foolish people.[21]

ઝ

Mos shkruaj gjë kur je i nervozuar sepse kur plaga e gjuhës është
më e keqe se e shpatës, mendo çfarë mund të jetë ajo e pendës?!
Never write when angry because if the wounds of the
tongue are greater than those of the sword, imagine
what the wounds of the pen will be?!

ઝ

Kot përpiqet mendja, kur nuk mund të arrijë gradën e lartë
të ndjenjave.
The human mind can try, but it can't reach the lofty
place of human emotion.

ઝ

---

21 I.e., why waste your time and mental strength with them.

*Fjala më elokuente është ajo, përfundimi i së cilës kuptohet që
në frazën e parë.*
The most eloquent speech is that which its message is
understood right from the beginning.

ଓଃ

*Tri raste kanë tri virtyte shumë të pëlqyeshme: t'i ndihmosh
nevojtarët kur janë në gjendje të vështirë; ta thuash të vërtetën
edhe kur je i zemëruar, të falësh kur je i zoti të ndëshkosh ose
të hakmerresh.*
Three instances have three very desirable virtues: to
help the needy when they are in distress, to tell the truth
even when angry or sad, to forgive when able
to retaliate.

ଓଃ

Për ndryshimin e një gjëje askush nuk është më i aftë se koha.
When it comes to change, no one is more capable and
experienced in this respect than time itself.

ଓଃ

Mahnitja, të shumtën e herës, lind nga injoranca.
Persiflage, most of the time, is born of ignorance.

*T'i japësh një pozitë dhe të nderosh një njeri pa merita, është
sikur të hedhësh në ndyrësira një qese me margaritarë.*
To put in a position of power a person without merits
is equal to throwing a pouch of pearls in the
waste dump.

ℭ

*Mos iu mbështet së nesërmes se nuk mund të dish se ç'do
të lindë nata!*
Do not count on tomorrow because you do not know
what the night will bring.

ℭ

*Liria s'mund të shkojë përpara, pa pasur udhëheqëse arsyen dhe
pa qenë e shoqëruar nga vetitë e mira.*
There is no progress in the pursuit of freedom unless
clear goals accompanied by good character lead
the way.

ℭ

Gjuha e memecit është më e mirë se e gënjeshtarit.
The speech of a mute person is more praiseworthy than
that of a liar.

ℭ

Sikundër trupi që ka nevojë për pastërti, ashtu edhe shpirti ka nevojë për arsim.
Like the human body is in need of purification, so is the soul in need of education.

ೞ

Pendimi është pranvera e mirësjelljes.
Repentance is the spring season of decency.[22]

ೞ

Një i menqur ka thën, "... Njerëzit e mëdhenj, të cilët me mendimet dhe punët e tyre kanë bërë të çuditet bota, a nuk ishin edhe ata njerëz si ne? Pse t'i shikoj ata me habi dhe mahnitje? A s'mund të bëhem edhe unë si ata me përpjekjet e mia?"
A wise one said "People are amazed by the achievements of great and knowledgeable individuals, but why should it be so? What did they have that you don't? Why can't you do the same if you too put in the effort?"[23]

ೞ

---

[22] I.e., repentance is key for a new beginning.
[23] This specific aphorism is indicated by Sami to have come from ancient Chinese philosophy.

Hidhërimi dhe gëzimi s'kanë kufi. Njeriut, pse ka zënë një pozitë të vogël, i bie pika nga gëzimi, pastaj ai vdes nga hidhërimi pse nuk zë një pozitë më të lartë.
Despair and joy have no limits. Man, because he occupies a small position, bursts out of joy, then he dies of bitterness because he does not occupy a higher position.

ɷ

Ai që e pëlqen veten e vet nuk pëlqehet nga askush.
He who is in love with himself is not loved by anyone else.

ɷ

Pasuria e vogël, që përdoret me nikoqirllëk, zë vend më mirë se thesaret e keq-administruar.
A small amount of wealth spent with care, is much better than a mismanaged treasure.

ɷ

Pasuria është shërbëtor i të mençurit, e zotëri i budallait.
Wealth is the servant of the wise, the master of the fool.

ɷ

*Lumturia në këtë botë i ngjan dritës së shkreptimës, ndriçimi i
një sekonde sjell pas furtunë disaorëshe.*
Happiness in this world resembles the flare of lightning,
a second of light is followed by hours of heavy thunder.

☙

Helmi më i rrezikshëm është hipokrizia.
The worst of poisons is hypocrisy.

☙

Dita është e shkurtër, puna e gjatë.
Days are short but work is not.

☙

*Njëri filozof i famshëm thotë: "S'mund t'i japësh flakë një pylli të
madh, po nuk të ndihmoi era". D.m.th. mos fillo punë të mëdha
po nuk qe koha dhe rasti dhe po nuk patë shpinë të fortë!*
A famous philosopher said "You can't set fire to a vast
forest if the wind isn't on your side," meaning never
start a fire too big that you cannot control.[24]

☙

---

[24] I.e., don't bite off more than you can chew. This specific
aphorism is indicated to have come from a Tibetan
philosopher.

Mos u prish me vëllanë për punë të shokut, sepse shoqëria zhduket, vëllazëria mbetet!
Do not sever your relationship with your brother because of a friend; friendships can dissolve but brotherhood lasts forever.

ॐ

Duke gërmuar tokën, del ujë.
Water comes out only when digging deep.[25]

ॐ

Virtytet e dijetarit të rënë në fatkeqësi duken më qartë.
The true virtues of a wise person are made clear when they are going through a hardship.[26]

ॐ

Ata që tregohen të drejtë me qëllim lartësimi, pasi të arrijnë qëllimin, s'ndjejnë më nevojë për drejtësi.
Those who present themselves as righteous in order to gain a position, once they achieve their goals, they see no need to be good or just.

---

[25] I.e., when performing a task, don't just scratch the surface.
[26] Their true nature becomes apparent by the manner in which they handle themselves during those difficult times.

ෆ

*Shërbimin që bën arsimi për përmirësimin e një kombi, ligji
s'mund ta bëjë kurrë.*
What education does in the improvement of a society,
no law can ever do.

ෆ

Shpagimi më i ëmbël është të bësh mirë së keqes që të është bërë.
The best way to repay a wrong done to you is to reply
to it with goodness.

ෆ

Kur lodhet trupi, qetësohet mendja.
When the (human) body gets tired, the mind
finds tranquility.

ෆ

Tregtia që të jep më shumë fitim është puna.
Hard work is the most profitable enterprise.

ෆ

Dituria është e gjatë, jeta e shkurtër.
Life is short but knowledge is limitless.

ᏟᏟ

Po të përdoret mirë koha, do të mjaftojë për të kryer çdo punë.
If time is taken advantage of wisely, it will suffice to
accomplish all daily tasks.[27]

ᏟᏟ

Çdo ditë e jetës sate është një faqe e jetëshkrimit tënd. Kujdesu ta
shkruash mirë sepse një faqe e keqe e ndynë gjithë librin.
Every day of your life is one page of your biography.
Write it with care because one bad page may stain
the whole book.

ᏟᏟ

Të qeshësh kundrejt një personi të dëshpëruar, është si t'ia heqësh
dikujt petkat në kohë të ftohtë dhe ta lësh lakuriq.
The worst thing you can do to a person in despair is to
make fun of their situation.

ᏟᏟ

---

[27] I.e., performing deep work.

*Do që të mos dëgjohet fjala që do të thuash? Mos e thuaj! Do që
të mos shihet puna që do të bësh? Mos e bëj!*
If you don't want your words to be heard, do not utter
them at all. If you don't want a [foul] deed to be seen,
simply do not do it.

ೞ

Po nuk foli i marri, nuk dallohet dot nga i urti.
If the fool stays quiet, no one would be able to tell him
apart from the wise one.

ೞ

Ndonjëherë, heshtja është më elokuente se çdo fjalë.
At times, silence is more eloquent than speech.

ೞ

*Një gjë e vogël e fituar me të drejtë është më e mirë se gjëja e
shumtë e fituar me të padrejtë.*
The smallest of things earned lawfully is a thousand
times better than the biggest of things earned
unlawfully.

ೞ

Bukuria e njeriut përbëhet nga bukuria e fjalës që flet.
The true beauty of a person is found in the words they speak.

ﬔ

Përgatite dyshekun para se të biesh të flesh!
Prepare your bed before going to sleep.[28]

ﬔ

Peri i ngatërruar nuk zgjidhet me nguti.
The tangled thread is not untangled in a hurry.[29]

ﬔ

Kush e ka barrën të rëndë, e ka hapin të shkurtër.
He who is carrying a heavy load can take only small steps.[30]

ﬔ

---

[28] I.e., make the necessary preparations for anything you hope to achieve.
[29] I.e., take your time in matters that require special attention.
[30] I.e., they are not able to do as much as they would like to due to their circumstances.

Njerëzit e mirë janë të gjykuar të bëhen skllevër të të këqijve.
Good people are designated to serve their
bad counterparts.[31]

෫

Lëmoje dhinë, pastaj mile.
First pat the goat, then milk it.[32]

෫

*Lumturia nuk zgjat për shumë kohë; i pafati është një foshnje në
bark të s'ëmës që ende s'ka arritur në botën e lumturisë; ndërsa
ai që është i lumtur, është një plak duke dhënë shpirt.*
Happiness does not last forever; unlucky is a baby in
the womb of her mother who has not yet arrived into
the world of happiness; while the one who is happy is
an old person who is about to leave this world.[33]

෫

---

[31] I.e., they are supposed to support and help them be better
people.

[32] I.e., begin all matters with kindness.

[33] I.e., this world is not as it seems, and that it and everything
in it is transient. The baby is in the darkness of the womb
only for a short time; they will soon see the light. And the
one who is already enjoying happiness will eventually leave
this world.

Qeveria (e mirë) lind nga rregulli dhe kujdesi.
Good government (i.e., leadership) is born of order
and care.

ങ

Njeriu duhet të përpiqet të mësojë çdo gjë, jo të tregojë veten e vet.
A person should try to learn everything he can, not to
show off himself.

ങ

Ato çka di njeriu, në krahasim me ato që nuk i di, është kurrgjë.
What one knows, compared to what he does not
know, is nothing.

ങ

*Askush s'mund të njihet për dijetar, pos atij që e mposht
epshin e vet.*
No one is wise, except for the one who overcomes his
own temptations.[34]

ങ

---

[34] This specific aphorism originates from a *hadith* of Prophet
Muhammad.

Dijetar është ai që i përshtatet puna fjalës së tij, e fjala opinionit të tij.

Wise is the one who says what he thinks and does what he says.

ℭ

Pasaniku koprrac i ngjan miut që rri në një tas të artë.

A stingy rich person resembles a mouse that sits in a golden bowl.[35]

ℭ

Njeriu që s'mund ta mbrojë mendimin e vet i ngjan një qyteti të pambrojtur.

A person that cannot defend his own ideas is like a defenseless city.

ℭ

---

[35] I.e., does nothing useful with his God-given resources.

Dijetari nuk thotë çka di kur nuk është rasti për t'i thënë,
i marri nuk di çka thotë.

A wise person does not say what he knows, if the
occasion does not call for it; whereas a fool does not
know what he says.[36]

૭

Më i forti i njerëzve është ai që është i zoti ta përmbajë vetveten.
The strongest of people are those who restrain
themselves (from acting hastily).[37]

૭

Lumturia (te njerëzit e ulët) shkakton kryelartësinë dhe
mospërfilljen ndaj të tjerëve.
Joy (in some wicked people) fosters a sense of pride
leading to disregard for others.

૭

---

[36] I.e. "Wise men speak because they have something
to say; fools because they have to say something"
wrote Plato.
[37] This specific aphorism originates from a *hadith* of Prophet
Muhammad.

*Mali lind vullkanin, vullkani çan malin, druri ushqen krimbin,
krimbi than drurin; njeriu krijon ide, idetë e fusin njeriun
në njëmijë fatkeqësira e më në fund e dërgojnë në
shtratin e veremit.*
Mountains give birth to volcanoes and volcanoes split
open the mountains; trees feed the worms and the
worms damage the trees; man comes up with ideas, and
his own ideas lead him to a thousand troubles, and
finally take him to the verge of melancholy.

ᘓ

*Përderisa ata që vdesin nga helmi janë fare të paktë, çdo njeri
trembet nga helmi, ndërsa shthurrja grin çdo ditë mijëra njerëz,
gjithkush jepet pas saj.*
While those who are killed by poison are very few,
everybody is afraid of poison and runs away from it,
while depravity destroys thousands of lives daily, people
still line up behind it.

ᘓ

*Gjithkush mendon për veten e tij, vetëm shpirtmiri mendon
për të tjerët.*
Everyone thinks for their own wellbeing, but the kind-
hearted people think for the wellbeing of others.

ᘓ

Po të fillosh një punë dhe të mos i dalësh në krye, mos u dëshpëro!
Po nuk ia dole me të parën, ia del me të dytën, dhe fundja
me të tretën.

If you start a task and are not able to complete it, do
not despair! If you did not succeed on the first try, give
it a second try, and even a third.[38]

೫

Mos u tremb nga shuplaka e mikut, duhet të kesh frikë nga
lëvdata e armikut.

Do not waver by the admonishment of your friend, you
should instead fear the praise given by your enemy.

೫

Në çdo mendim mund të ketë shkarje e në çdo veprim gabim;
mendimet korrigjohen me kohë, veprimet me përvojë.

In every thought there may be slippage, and error in
action; thoughts are corrected with time, actions
with experience.

೫

---

[38] I.e., never give up.

Shumë rrallë i takon fatkeqësia atij që, kur del në mëngjes nga shtëpia, i shkon mendja se në mbrëmje mund të kthehet me qivur (arkivol).
Disaster rarely strikes a person who leaves his house in the morning mindful that in the evening he might return in a casket.[39]

ଔ

Gjithë ç'është në botë, me shpirt dhe pa shpirt, është armik i njeriut; njeriu i urtë qëndron gjithmonë me kujdes dhe nuk ka besim në asnjeri, në asgjë.
All that exists, with or without a soul, is an enemy to man; a wise person is always cautious of this and trusts no one, and nothing.

ଔ

Ç'mund të bëjë një kalë i fortë me një karrocë të shkatërruar?
What can a strong horse do with a broken carriage?[40]

ଔ

---

[39] I.e., he or she is always mindful and prepared for the inevitable.
[40] I.e., context and circumstances matter.

Më kryesoret janë katër gjëra që e bëjnë njeriun njeri: dituria, durimi, kanaati (mjaftimi me atë që ka) dhe drejtësia.
Four things of utmost importance that make a person human are: knowledge, patience, contentment, and justice.

ଔ

Uji në vetvete është i pastër, duke u trazuar me disa materie dhe sende të tjera, bëhet i hidhur dhe i ndyrë; njeriu është krijuar i mirë, bëhet i keq nga ndikimi i epsheve dhe i veseve të këqija.
Water in its original state is pure, when its mode of being is disturbed it becomes dirty; man is created good, becomes evil from the influences of lust and bad vices.

ଔ

Njeriu dëshiron të jetojë shumë, por nuk dëshiron të plaket.
People wish to live long lives, but detest getting old.

ଔ

Nga një birucë e vogël, mund të hyjë një e keqe e madhe.
A minor opening can give way to great corruption.[41]

---

[41] A minor corruption, no matter how small, can give way to greater ones.

Sikur çdo njeri t'i konsiderojë të gjithë njerëzit për shokë, gratë — përveç të tijën — si nëna dhe motra, atëherë është e mundshme të ketë lumturi dhe prehje në këtë botë.

If people (men) viewed everyone as their friends and women as their mothers and sisters, only then will it be possible to find happiness and peace in this world.

ଔ

Po deshe ta kesh të lirë zemrën tënde, mos i plotëso dëshirat (e këqija)!

If you wish to be free (of worry),[42] do not fulfill your (evil) temptations.

ଔ

Mos jep shkas të flasë kush keq për ty; por mos u mundo t'ua mbyllësh gojën keqdashësve, sepse qeni, ashtu sikundër i leh natën kusarit që i kalon pranë, ashtu i leh edhe njeriut të ndershëm.

Give no excuse to anyone to speak ill of you, and if they do, don't try to shut the mouths of the evil-doers, because the dog, just as it barks at the robber passing by at night, so it does with the honest person.[43]

ଔ

---

[42] I.e., in this world and the next.

[43] I.e., evil-doers and backbiters will speak ill of others, no matter how good or bad the others are.

Po të flitet keq për ndokënd, gjithsecili beson në çast; po të flitet mirë për të, asnjeri nuk beson. Përçarja është bërë aq e pëlqyer në botë, saqë lëvdatës nuk i ka mbetur fare vlerë.

If someone is badly talked about, others immediately believe it. If one speaks good about that same person, no one believes it. Strife and animosity have become so popular in our world that praise no longer holds any value.

Smiraku e grindaveci edhe sikur ta zotërojnë tërë botën, prapë s'mund të kënaqen, sepse për t'u bërë ata të lumtur, duhet të shkatërrohet gjithë bota.

The jealous person and the quarreler will never be satisfied, even if they owned the whole world; for them to be happy, the whole world must be destroyed.

Martesa është një urë midis shthurjes dhe lumturisë.
Marriage is a bridge between depravity and happiness.[44]

---

[44] I.e., it saves people from many vices.

Ekzistenca dhe lumturia e shoqërisë njerëzore varet nga gruaja.
Midani thotë: "Aty ku mungon gruaja, asaj duhet bërë një
shtatore prej druri".
Human existence and happiness depend on women.
Tradition holds that "where there is no woman, there
should be a statue in her place."[45]

ભ

Nuk i besohet premtimit të atij që premton shumë.
Never trust the person who makes too many promises.

ભ

Lëvdata e bën njeriun të kthehet nga rruga që ka zënë, kurse
kritika e bën ta kontrollojë rrugën e vet dhe ta vazhdojë.
Praising someone can make them change their
direction,[46] however, criticising them will make them
evaluate their direction and continue on it.

ભ

---

[45] A figurative statue; i.e., women should be involved in every
level of society for it to achieve peace, tranquility, and
success. This is also an indication of the great status of
women in Islam as understood by Sami Frashëri.
[46] I.e., get a big head.

Personi që do ti, s'ka asnjë të metë, fillo të mos e duash, shih sa të meta ka.

The person you are in love with is flawless, if you stop being in love with them, you will see all of their flaws and imperfections.[47]

03

Gjithsecili mban në gojë punën e të pasurve; vetëm njeriu zemërmirë mendon gjithmonë gjendjen e të varfërve.

Most people concern themselves with the matters of the rich, but good-hearted people concern themselves with the matters of the poor.[48]

03

Ujët që pihet me ngadalë, largon etjen më shumë.

Water drunk slowly quenches thirst faster.

03

Ngutja në marrjen e vendimeve në çështje të vështira dhe të dyshimta, është e dëmshme.

Haste when deciding complex and doubtful matters is harmful.

---

[47] I.e., love is blind.
[48] I.e., help them.

ରଟ

Kush nuk është i gjykuar, është gjykues.
He who has not been judged himself tends to
judge others.

ରଟ

Kush kuvendon me botën, kuvendon me persona të zakonshëm;
kush lexon libra, kuvendon me filozofë, letrarë dhe me njerëz
të famshëm.
Whoever consults the world, consults regular people;
whoever reads books, consults philosophers, academics
and famous people.

ରଟ

Zbavitja më e bukur për njëriun është leximi, shoku më
i mirë është libri.
Reading is the best form of entertainment; a book is
the best of friends.

ରଟ

Kush çmon (lëvdon) një ligësi, është më i lig se ai që e bën.
Whoever praises an evil deed is worse than the person
who commits such a deed.

ରଟ

Hiq dorë nga ligësia edhe ajo heq dorë nga ti.
Abandon malice and it will abandon you.

ℭ

Çdo mizor e ka ditën e vet të gjykimit.
Every cruel person has his own day of judgment.[49]

ℭ

Në qoftë se pret të vijë koha për t'i bërë mirë njerëzisë, asnjëherë s'ke për t'i bërë mirë.
If you wait for the perfect time to help people, you will never be able to perform any such good deeds.[50]

ℭ

S'ka lumturi më të madhe në botë se dashuria dhe harmonia.
There is no greater happiness in this world than love and harmony (among people).

ℭ

---

[49] I.e., they will one day pay for what they have done.
[50] I.e., the perfect time may never come.

*Buka thatë, që hahet me dashuri dhe bashkim, është më e
këndshme se gostitë me mëri e kundërshtim.*
Bread alone eaten with fellowship and love, is more
pleasant than any feasting with grudges and contempt.

 C3

Hileja s'mund ta mundë kurrë të vërtetën.
Cheating can never prevail over the truth.

C3

*Babai që neglizhon edukimin e së bijës, përgatit turpin e vet dhe
shkatërimin e dhëndrit të tij.*
A father that neglects the education of his daughter
prepares shame for himself and hurts his son-in-law.[51]

C3

*Ajo që qeveris botën nuk është as forca, as ligji, por është
mirësjellja dhe edukata.*
That which rules the world is not power or law but
decency and civility.

C3

---

[51] I.e., invest in your child's education as it will pay off later.

*Një komb endacak me moral të shëndoshë është një mijë herë më i
pëlqyer se një komb i qytetëruar me moral të prishur.*
A poor and aimless nation with sound morality is a
thousand times better than a civilized nation with
corrupt morals.

ര

*Dijetari nuk ndjek çdo zakon të vendit të tij, por përpiqet për
zhdukjen e zakoneve të liga të bashkëkombësve të tij.*
A wise person does not follow every custom of his own
people, instead he tries to get rid of the wicked
traditions among his people.

ര

*Trathtari ikën si dhelpra, pa qenë i ndjekur nga askush; i drejti,
edhe sikur ta rrethojë gjithë bota, qëndron me kurajo të plotë si
luan dhe nuk tundet nga vendi.*
The traitor runs away like a fox even if no one is after
him; a just person, even if cornered by all of humanity,
like a lion stands his ground courageous and
unwavering.[52]

ര

---

[52] This specific aphorism seems to have been derived from
Qur'anic injunctions like 6:17-18, 10:107, and others.

Një shtëpi po ta ketë themelin e dobët, prapëseprapë qëndron
për ca kohë, por po nuk pati dashuri ndërmjet njerëzve,
që janë në të, shembet.
Even if a house has a weak foundation, it will still stand
firm for some time, but if there is no love between the
people who live in it, it will soon crumble.

☙

Njeriu njeh për të mendshëm vetëm ata që janë dakord me
mendimin e tij.
Often people see as being wise only those who agree
with them.

☙

Lumturia e pleqve është të shohin fëmijët e fëmijëve të tyre që
kanë sjellë në botë.
The happiness of the elderly often comes from seeing
their grandchildren enter this world.

☙

Nderimi i tepëruar është njëfarë përbuzje.
Excessive reverence is a form of sacrilege.

☙

Në botë nuk gjënden dy mendime të ngjashme nga çdo pikëpamje;
ai që pranon çdo mendim të filozofëve më të mëdhenj pa
kundërshtuar asnjërin, është pa mend.
In this world, no two opinions are the same in every
way; a person who accepts every opinion of the great
people without questioning any of them is a fool.[53]

ଓ

Një punë e bukur është më e dobishme se një mijë fjalë të bukura.
A good deed performed is better than a thousand good
words spoken.

ଓ

Fëmija sikundër që mëson të flasë gjuhën e s'ëmës, t'atit dhe të
gjindve të tjerë të shtëpisë, pajiset edhe me moralin e tyre.
Just like the child learns the language of her mother,
father and other people of the house, she also takes on
their morals.

ଓ

Nuk është mësuesi ai që edukon njeriun, por nëna.
It's not the teacher who educates a child, it is
the mother.

---

[53] I.e., fact check your information, no matter the
source.

∞

*Kënaqësia e zbavitjeve dhe e lojërave është në shoqëri, kënaqësia
e leximit në vetmi.*
The pleasure of entertainment and play is found with
friends; the pleasure of reading is found in solitude.

∞

*Njeriu e shikon të shkuarën me ngashërim, të ardhmen me
shpresë; asnjëherë nuk është i kënaqur nga e tashmja.*
People look at their past with grief, the future with
hope, and are never pleased with the present.

∞

*Lumturia i ngjan hënës që duket në majën e një mali; njeriu thot:
po të dal në majën e këtij mali do ta kap hënën; mirëpo kalon sa
fusha e sa male — përsëri hënën e shikon të qëndrojë në majë të
malit tjetër që ka përpara.*
Happiness resembles the moon over the top of a
mountain; man says: if I can only get to the other side
of the mountain, I will catch the moon; he passes many
mountains and fields chasing it and still sees the moon
standing over the top of the next mountain.

∞

Njeriu është gjuetar i shpresës; duke u turrur pas saj, bie në gropë, ndërsa shpresa fluturon, ikën.
Man is the hunter of hope; he hurls after it, and in the process falls in a pit, while hope flies away.

ভ

Njeriu nuk dëshprohet për fatkeqësinë dhe mizerjen që ka pësuar, por hidhërohet duke e kujtuar lumturinë e tij të humbur.
People often aren't as sad for what has presently befallen them as much as they are when thinking of their past lost happiness.

Appendix A
The Albanian Alphabet & Transliteration Chart

Letters		Read	Pronounce	Albanian Examples	English equivalent
A	a	a	a	afër	f<u>a</u>r
B	b	bë	b	bukë	<u>b</u>at
C	c	cë	ts	ceremoni	i<u>ts</u>y
Ç	ç	çë	tʃ	çelës	<u>ch</u>at
D	d	dë	d	dasëm	<u>d</u>oor
Dh	dh	dhë	ð	dhelpër	<u>th</u>ere
E	e	e	e	emër	<u>e</u>nter
Ë	ë	ë	ə	ëmbël	<u>a</u>round
F	f	fë	f	fletë	<u>f</u>ly
G	g	gë	g	gurë	<u>g</u>um
Gj	gj	gjë	ɟ	gjeneral	<u>j</u>oin
H	h	hë	h	hap	<u>h</u>at
I	i	i	i	ilaç	s<u>ea</u>

J	j	jë	j	javë	yawn
K	k	kë	k	këmishë	kite
L	l	lë	l	lopë	leave
Ll	ll	llë	ł or l	llampë	mill
M	m	më	m	mal	man
N	n	në	n	nënë	no
Nj	nj	një	ɲ	njeri	onion
O	o	o	o	orë	open
P	p	së	p	parti	pen
Q	q	që	q	qumësht	mature
R	r	rë	ɾ	raport	red
Rr	rr	rrë	r (rolled)	rrjesht	borrow
S	s	së	s	stacion	stop
Sh	sh	shë	ʃ	shtëpi	Shop

T	**t**	të	t	televizion	<u>t</u>ree
Th	**th**	thë	θ	thupër	<u>th</u>in
U	**u**	u	u	urë	f<u>oo</u>d
V	**v**	vë	v	vezë	<u>v</u>est
X	**x**	xë	dz	xixë	ad<u>ze</u>
Xh	**xh**	xhë	dȝ	xhaxha	<u>J</u>upiter
Y	**y**	y	y	yll	n<u>ew</u>*
Z	**z**	z	z	zemër	<u>z</u>ebra
Zh	**zh**	zhë	ȝ	zhurmë	plea<u>s</u>ure

*No English equivalent found. Equivalent to *mons<u>ieu</u>r* in French.

Appendix B
Glossary of Albanian Terms

English	Albanian
Albania	Shqipëria
Albanian (lang.)	shqip
bird	zog
book	libër
brother	vëlla
castle	kështjellë; kala
country	shtet/vend
daughter	vajzë
day	ditë
dictionary	fjalor
English	anglisht
earth	tokë
fall/autumn	vjeshtë
father	baba
fire	zjarr

flower	lule
forest	pyll
game	lojë
hello	tungjatjeta
history	histori
hour	orë
house	shtëpi
hot	nxehtë
husband	bashkëshort
lake	liqen
language	gjuhë
library	bibliotekë
moon	hënë
no	jo
office	zyrë
people	njerëz; popull
rain	shi
foot	këmbë

river	lumë
sea	det
sky	qiell
snow	borë
son	djalë; bir
spring	pranverë
summer	verë
star	yll
time	kohë
tree	pemë
wife	bashkëshorte
winter	dimër
yes	po
God	Zot

Appendix C
Chronology of Albanian History[54]

334-323 BCE – Alexander the Great controls the region

168 BCE – Romans conquer Illyria

547 CE – First Slavic invasions in the region begin

850s – Kosova (then Dardania) is absorbed by the Bulgarian Empire

700-800s – Slavic tribes invade Illyrian lands and start settling the region

1018 – The region becomes part of Byzantium

1184-1196 – Under Stefan Nemanja I, the Serbs expand from Rascia into eastern Kosova

1208-1216 – With the conquest of Prizren under Stefan Nemanja II most of Kosova falls under Serbian rule

1219-1300s – The period under the rule of the Serbian principality of Rascia witnesses the building of Serbian

---

[54] See *The Book of Albanian Sayings*, Trans. F. Vehapi.

Orthodox churches and monasteries across Kosova and the region

1345-1371 – Ottomans appear in the Balkans

1389 – Armies from the Balkans (Serbs, Albanians, Bosnians, and others) under King Lazar are defeated at the Battle of Kosova (the Field of Blackbirds) by the Ottomans under the rule of Sultan Murad I

1396-1423 – Elements of Ottoman administration are set up in various parts of Kosova

1443 – Skanderbeg rebels and fights back the Ottomans

1448 – Second Battle of Kosova consolidates Ottoman rule in the Balkans

1453 – Sultan Mehmet Fatih conquers Constantinople (and names it *Istanbul*); Albania and Kosova become provinces of the Ottoman Empire

1467 – The Albanian Kingdom comes under direct control of the Ottomans enjoying internal autonomy

1521 – Sultan Suleiman the Magnificent conquers Belgrade (the capital of Serbia)

1600-1700 – The majority of Albanians willingly convert to Islam because of the great Ottoman example, and some in order to be exempt from paying the *jizya* (per capita tax on non-Muslims of a Muslim state)

1689 – A Habsburg army conquers Kosova but are shortly forced to withdraw

1737 – Habsburg forces capture Prishtina but weeks later abandon Kosova

1785 – Kara Mahmud Pasha Bushatliu of Shkodra captures most of Kosova

1877-1878 – The Ottomans lose foothold in Serbia, Montenegro and Bulgaria because of the Russo-Ottoman war; Serbs expel some 50,000 Muslims to Kosova from the Sanjak of Niš

1878 – Serbs occupy parts of Kosova; Treaty of San Stefano give parts of Kosova to Serbia and Montenegro; The League of Prizren (made up of mostly Muslim delegates) meets in Prizren in response to the treaty; The League also demands autonomy of Albania within Ottoman rule

1880 – The League of Prizren controls most of Kosova

1881 – Ottoman forces disperse the League and reclaim most of Kosova

1903-1912 – Albanian uprisings against the Young Turks take place in various cities of Kosova and beyond

1912 – The First Balkan War; Albania declares independence from the Ottomans; Serbs occupy Kosova

1913 – Kosova becomes part of the Kingdom of Serbia; estimated that 25,000 Albanians killed during Serb invasion

1915 – Bulgarian troops invade parts of Kosova

1918 – Kosova is retaken by Serbs

1919 – Serbs pillage throughout Kosova and kill over 6,000 Kosovar Albanians

1928 – The number of Serb colonists introduced to Kosova by the Serbian government is raised from 24 percent in 1919 to 38 percent

1929 – The Kingdom of the Serbs, Croats of Slovenes now is called Yugoslavia; Kosova is brought under Yugoslav rule

1933-1935 – The Yugoslav government begins the deportation of the Muslim Albanian communities to Turkey; the Yugoslav government begins confiscation of lands belonging to the local Kosovar Albanians

1937 – Serbian Vaso Čubrilović writes the secret memorandum "Expulsion of Albanians," advocating for a forced removal of all Albanians from Kosova who are around 90% Muslim

1939 – Italy invades Albania; Albania rescues 100 percent of the Jewish population there during WWII

1941 – Josip Tito organizes the partisan movement in Yugoslavia; Kosova becomes part of the Italian-controlled Albania; Enver Hoxha takes lead of the Communist Party

1943 – Germany invades Albania

1944 – Communists in Albania establish provisional

government and appoint Enver Hoxha as Prime
Minister

1945 – Churchill gives Kosova, Macedonia, Slovenia
and Croatia to Communist Yugoslavia under the rule of
Tito; Yugoslavia introduces military rule in Kosova;
religious communities suffer a reign of terror

1945-1951 – Thousands of Kosovar Albanians are
murdered and expelled to Turkey after being labeled as
"Turks" because of their shared faith with the majority
of Turkish people

1948-1950 – Yugoslav-Albanian relations fall apart;
borders are sealed

1946 – Kosova is absorbed into the Yugoslav
federation; Socialist People's Republic of Albania is
proclaimed

1961 – Albania allies itself with China

1948 – Tito breaks with USSR

1968 – First demonstrations for independence in
Kosova, during which many were arrested

1974 - The Yugoslavian constitution declares Kosova an Autonomous Province of Yugoslavia

1980 – Yugoslav leader Tito dies; Serbs begin their campaign to retake Kosova from Albanians and make it a province of Greater Serbia

1981 – Kosovar Albanian students at the University of Prishtina begin rioting in defense of Kosovar Albanian rights; hundreds of peaceful Kosovar demonstrators are wounded and killed

1981-1989 – The Serbian campaign against Kosovar Albanians intensifies. Hundreds of students are poisoned by the food given to them at their schools

1985 – Albania's dictator, Enver Hoxha, dies

1989 – Serbian leader Slobodan Milošević rallies thousands of Serbs at the Field of Blackbirds to remind them that Serbs will never give up Kosova, "the Heart of Serbia," and that the economical and political sufferings of the Serbs in Kosova are because of the high constitutional status of the Albanians in Yugoslavia

1989-1990 – Milošević takes away Kosova's constitutional status as an autonomous province and reduces the country to an integral part of Serbia. Milošević abolishes the Assembly of Kosova and dissolves its government. Kosovar employees are fired. The campaign for the closing of all Albanian schools begins. The Albanian-speaking media is silenced; health services and other institutional funds for Albanians are usurped

1991 – The Yugoslav Federation is dissolved; the European Community (now European Uunion) establishes an Arbitration Commission to make decisions regarding recognition of its former constituents as independent countries. This Commission accepts Slovenia's and Croatia's applications, but not that of Bosnia or Kosova

1992 – Albania's Democratic Party wins elections, and Salih Berisha becomes president. In Kosova, Ibrahim Rugova, an advocate of non-violence, is elected the first president of the Republic of Kosova; unofficial referendum among ethnic Albanians in Macedonia shows overwhelming wish for their own territorial autonomy; Bosnia holds its referendum and 99 percent of the ballots come in favor of independence. However,

at the time, the Serbian government was preparing for
the slaughter of thousands of Bosnian Muslims

1992-1995 – Serbian extremists carry out genocide in
Bosnia. In July of 1995, two years after being declared a
"Safe Haven" by the UN, around 8,000 Bosnian
Muslims are massacred in Srebrenica

1995 – Talks are held at Dayton, Ohio, to resolve the
Balkan crisis. Bosnia is divided into a Serb and a
Muslim-Croat federation

1996-97 – Hate-filled Serbian nationalist, Vojislav Šešelj,
publicly advocates infecting Kosovar Albanians with
the AIDS virus; the Kosova Liberation Army (KLA)
emerges as a reaction to the presence of the Serbian
regime throughout Kosova

1997 – Unrest in Albania brings the Socialists to power;
Serbian military offensive increases tremendously in
Kosova; U.S. and E.U. diplomats are repeatedly
deceived by Milošević's false promises to end his
campaign of ethnic cleansing

1998 – Milošević and Rugova hold talks for the first
time but without any results; Serbian forces attack
central Kosova, killing many Albanian civilians;

international diplomacy fails; NATO allies airstrike Serbian military targets; in October, Milošević agrees to withdraw troops and allow refugees to return, and Belgrade agrees to allow 2,000 unarmed international monitors to verify compliance; envoy Christopher Hill tries to broker political settlement, but violence undermines cease-fire

1999 – In January, 45 Albanian men were killed in Racak and 24 more were killed later that month; the Western allies demand peace talks from both sides or face airstrikes; in February, both parties met in Rambouliett, France; that month Serbian forces attack KLA positions and KLA fights back; in March, Kosovar Albanian leaders sign the peace deal which gave them a "broad interim autonomy" and 28,000 NATO troops to keep the peace. The deal also requires the disbandment of the KLA, but surprisingly Serbian authorities refuse the deal, and this suspends the talks

1999 – On March 20, international peace monitors evacuate Kosova while NATO prepares to start bombardments; on the 22nd Richard Holbrooke warns Milošević of airstrikes for the last time, but Milošević still refuses to allow NATO troops in Kosova; on the 24th airstrikes against Serbian military targets begin;

Serbian atrocities continue against Kosovar Albanian civilians

1999 – In April, over 600,000 Kosovar Albanians are forced to leave their homes during NATO airstrikes, their properties are looted and homes are burned; thousands of people are murdered; the Western allies refuse to arm the KLA because of the arms embargo placed on Yugoslavia; by May Serbian troops increase in Kosova and over a million Kosovar Albanians are expelled; Milošević is indicted for war crimes by the International Criminal Tribune

1999 – In June, NATO's 72-day airstrike campaign ends the Serbian occupation of Kosova; UN Security Council passes the Security Council Resolution 1244 placing Kosova under transitional UN administration (UNMIK)

2000 – Now declared a war criminal, Milošević runs again for president, but loses national elections in Serbia

2001-2002 – Because of its considerable Albanian population there, Macedonian parliament recognizes Albanian as an official language

2002 – At the Hague, Milošević's trial begins; he dies four years later at the Hague

2003 – The Socialist Party wins in Albania

2006 – In January, President Rugova dies and is succeeded by Fatmir Sejdiu; in October, Serbian voters in a referendum in Serbia approve a new constitution which declares Kosova an integral part of Serbia, and Kosovar Albanians boycott the ballot

2007 – In February, the UN envoy Martti Ahtisaari unveils the plan to set Kosova on its road to independence, and Serbia and Russia reject it

2008 – On February 17, Kosova declares independence, but Serbia rejects it, calling it illegal under international law; in April, Kosova's parliament adopts new constitution; in December, the E.U. mission (Eulex) takes over police, justice and customs services from the UN in Kosova; Macedonia recognizes Kosova's independence

2009 – Albania joins NATO

2010 – In response to Serbian claims, the UN

International Court of Justice rules that Kosova's declaration of independence was not illegal under any international law

2012 – Period of Kosova's international supervision of independence ends

2015-2017 – Middle Eastern refugees appear in the Balkans making their way to northern Europe

Frasheri's Portraits

Fig. 1. Sami Frashëri's portrait on Albanian stamp, 1950.

Fig. 2. Portrait of the Frashëri brothers, 1865.

Fig. 3. Sami Frashëri during his time as the editor-in chief of 'Tercuman-i Sark,' Istanbul, date unknown.

Fig. 4. Frashëri's portrait commonly found in the
Middle East, date unknown.

Fig. 5. Frashëri's portrait in Ottoman attire, date unknown.

Fig. 6. Frashëri at work, date unknown.

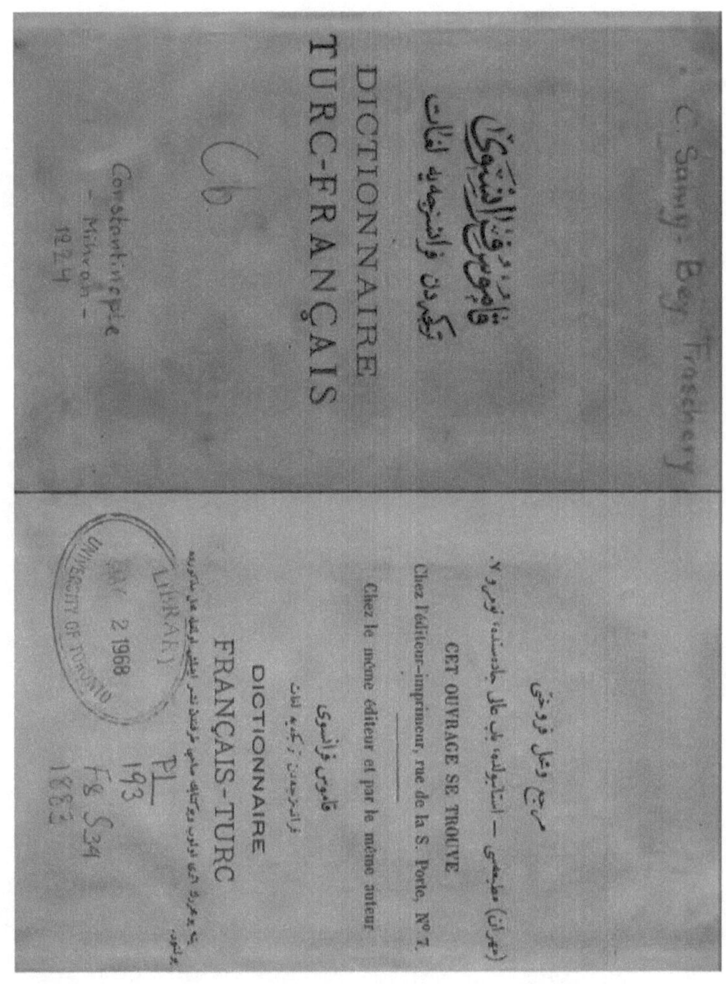

Fig. 7. Frashëri's *Kamus-i Fransevi* (French-Turkish dictionary), 1883 edition.

Bibliography and Suggested Readings

Bilmez, Bülent. "Shemseddin Sami Frashëri (1850–1904): Contributing to the Construction of Albanian and Turkish Identities." *We, the People*, edited by Diana Mishkova, Central European University Press, 2009, p. 341–371.

Dağlıoğlu, Hikmet Turhan. *Semsettin Sami Bey: hayatı ve eserleri*. Resimli Ay Matbaası, 1934.

Elsie, Robert. *Albanian Alphabets: Borrowed and Invented*. CS Publishing, 2017.

____. *Historical Dictionary of Albania* (2nd Ed.). Scarecrow Press, 2010.

"Fjalë Të Urta." *Jeta e Re*, n. 3, 1978.

Frashëri, Şemseddin Sami. *Himmat al-himam fiy nashr al-Islam*. Mihran Matbaası, 1885.

____. *Medeniyyet-i İslamiyye,* (Cep Kütüphanesi, Aded: 1), Mihran Matbaası, 1879.

____. *Kamus-ul Alam: Tarih Ve Cografya Lugati Ve Tabir-I Esahhiyle Kaffe-yi Esma-yi Hassa-yi Camidir*. Mihran Matbaası, 1889.

____. *"Lisan ve Edebiyatımız" Tercüman-I Hakikat ve Musavver*

Servet-I Fünün, Kırkambar ve Alem Matbaaları. Mihran Matbaası, 1889.

___. *Përpjekjet e Heronjëve në Përhapjen E Islamit*. Trans. I. Ahmedi. Logos-A, 2003.

___. *Qyteterimi Islam*. N. T. Logos-A, 2009.

Frashëri, Sami, and Zija Xholi, et al. *Vepra 1 & 2*. Shtypshkronja e Re Tiranë, 1988.

Furat , Ayse Z. & Hamit Er (Eds). *Balkans and Islam: Encounter, Transformation, Discontinuity, Continuity*. Cambridge Scholars Publishing, 2012.

Gawrych, George Walter. *The Crescent And The Eagle*. I.B. Tauris, 2006.

Hanson, Matt. "Scribes and Bibliophiles: Müteferrika to Modernity at the Bodleian Library." *Daily Sabah*, 29 Mar. 2018, *https://www.dailysabah.com/books/2018/03/30/ scribes-and-bibliophiles-muteferrika-to-modernity-at-the-bodleian- library*, http://www.website.com.

Itzkowitz, Norman. *Ottoman Empire and Islamic Tradition*. Phoenix Book, 1980.

Khan, Muhammad Mojlum. *Great Muslims Of The West*. Kube Publishing Ltd, 2017.

Malcolm, Noel. *Agents Of Empire*. Penguin Books, 2016.

McCarthy, Justin. *Death and Exile: The Ethnic Cleansing of Ottoman Muslims, 1821-1922.* Darwin Press, 1995.

Levend, Agâh Sirri. *Türk Dilinde Gelişme ve Sadeleşme Evreleri.* Türk Tarih Kurumu, 1960.

Lough, James, and Alex Stein, editors. *Short Circuits.* Schaffner Press, 2018.

"Sami Frashëri." *Gjuha Shqipe*, 17 Dec. 2016, http://www.gjuhashqipe.com/sq/Figura-te-Albanologjise/Sami-Frash%C3%ABri.

Şemseddin Sami Fraşeri. (2018). In: *Encyclopædia Britannica.* [online] Encyclopædia Britannica, Inc. Available at: https://www.britannica.com/biography/Semseddin-Sami-Fraseri [Accessed 29 Nov. 2018].

"Thënie Të Sami Frashërit." *Telegrafi*, Spring 2018, *https://telegrafi.com/thenie-te-sami-frasherit-duhen-shume-mend-qe-te-mund-shoqerohesh-njerez-pa-mend/,* http://www.website.com.

Acknowledgments

All praise and gratitude belong to the Creator who enabled me to translate this rare work of classical Albanian and Ottoman literature. There are numerous distinguished individuals I wish to thank and acknowledge for their tremendous support with this work and that includes my family, friends and mentors. First of all, many thanks to Carol Ledford, Christie King and Ilir Bekteshi for proofreading this translation. Countless thanks to the following friends and mentors for their help and support in many of my endeavors: Burhan Fili, Didmar Faja, Abdullah Alkadi, Joel Hayward, Jon Mandaville, and Amber Haque. My deepest gratitude also goes to Masud and Salma Ahmad, Mike and Linda Tresemer, Maqsood and Eloisa Chaudhary, Usman Mughal, Azim Haque, Kaan Katircioglu, Rania Ayoub, Imran Maqbool, Ahmed Al-Baloushi, Mohammad Al-Rashdi, Ilir Bekteshi, Ali and Aziz Govori, Fadil Mourad, Shahidul Haque, Dana Lundell, and the following families: Brady and Wright, Bresa, Yavuz, Obaidi, Mirza, Jaffar, Gashi, Carter, Beaton, and many more.

About the Translator

Flamur Vehapi is a researcher, poet, literary translator, academic and a leadership and success coach. He received his A.A. and B.S. in Counseling Psychology with a minor in History, and in 2013, he received his M.A. from Portland State University in Conflict Resolution. Currently, he is an Education and Leadership PhD student at Pacific University. Flamur taught social sciences at Rogue Community College and Southern Oregon University, and more recently he taught at various institutions in the Middle East. His publications include *The Alchemy of Mind* and *A Cup with Rumi*, both collections of spiritual poems, and his most recent books are *Peace and Conflict Resolution in Islam, The Book of Albanian Sayings* and *The Book of Great Quotes,* and two translations of Sami Frashëri's books. Flamur and his family currently live in Oregon, USA.

About the Type

The text of this book was set in Garamond. Garamond is a group of many old-style serif typefaces, named for sixteenth-century Parisian engraver Claude Garamond. Garamond-style typefaces are popular and used often, particularly for printing body text and books.

Notes